"BECOME YOURSELF" WORKBOOK STUDENT JOURNAL

LIFE SKILLS / LIFE STUDIES

We can learn from African culture and heritage!

CLASSROOM SETS

STORY BY JEOFFREY BEST

Biography / Facts

TEXT & VERSE BY WENDE BEST

Narrative, Pep Talks, Heritage

Culture & Vocabulary

authorHOUSE®

AuthorHouse™
1663 Liberty Drive
Bloomington, IN 47403
www.authorhouse.com
Phone: 1-800-839-8640

Published by AuthorHouse   10/23/2012

ISBN: 978-1-4772-8029-4 (sc)
ISBN: 978-1-4772-8028-7 (e)

Jeoffrey Best Copyright permission by Olan Mills

FOREWORD

Wende Best has presented her copyrighted plays, poetry, songs and workshops since 1987.

Ms. Best has provided opportunities for many people; including individuals, organizations and youth groups. This workbook is a combination of values, culture, personal revelations and narrative. She invites the reader to journal beside the story of the experience of Jeoffrey Best, told in verse. His story takes place in the suburbs. "We did not live ghetto stereotypes of drugs and gangs, or . . . the popular images of privilege and perfection, away from the inner cities."

In this edition, we are examining lives side by side—appreciating another's personal journey. Each scenario is an example. The goal is to document the productivity of people for a cohesive and stable environment. That is the world view of Wende Best and Jeoffrey Best. Each person reaches for the best that can be realized in their own dreams and desires, that are different from theirs, yet have the common elements that drive every human being.

Jeoffrey Best was born in a North Hollywood mansion, turned Boys Home—

the back story in Hollywood lingo . . .

"Become Yourself" is a story of aspiring! Struggle with a divorced/single parent; has tragic incidents, including a few days of homelessness. A day late, a dollar short—dealing with financial crisis. Determined, dedicated and finally, a triumphant—happy ending!

This book is a project for a DVD, Radio Play and CD.

Dramatized by music, sound effects and character voices.

No Generation Gap Radio Show © Radio Play CD Compilation

"Become Yourself" Workbook—2nd Printing

About The Book

The purpose of "Become Yourself" Workbook is inspiration and motivation.

Wende Best is releasing this edition of "Become Yourself" Workbook—Student Journal for her son's 35th birthday. He became a symbol of hope to15 year old juveniles, when he was born into a group home. Wende and her husband were the House-Parents to six delinquent teenagers. "The new baby in the house made it a real home." The administration of the *mansion*, as it was referred to, was the start of enriching the community.

As Jeoffrey grew up, he willingly and eagerly participated in a long list of projects by helping his mother (and grandmother) in a lifestyle of community service. Tragically, during one fund-raising event for dying children of Africa, he endured a severe guard dog attack inside a downtown Los Angeles restaurant, due to the negligence of the owner. Nonetheless, by 15 years old, Jeoffrey has an impressive resume, and makes a difference in the lives of others, as recognized by a Commendation from President Bill Clinton. Jeoffrey Best knows the value of giving.

Jeoffrey's destiny is symbolic of the community. This book is his legacy. Bad things can happen to good people. The challenge is to remain faithful. Stay true to yourself. Continue to care and to do extraordinary things in spite of adversity. "Doing good makes you feel good." *You can develop the best for your life, through character, life studies and standards.*

The process of negotiation with basketball star Shaquille O'Neal's management established a new position in their organization for Jeoffrey, as the first official correspondent in Los Angeles. This demonstrates faith to persevere. He achieved his dream. He became part of the professional basketball community. The agency remarked that *Jeoffrey's sports writing ability and talent rivaled any professional, twice his age.* Currently, he writes an online sports Blog and newsletter.

Jeoffrey achieved all of his goals by18; including early entrance to college at 16, but he became ill with a brain disorder. His college (degree) and potential adult career was interrupted. He takes medication and therapeutic classes to manage his condition. Jeoffrey Best and Wende Best have collaborated on many projects.

"Become Yourself" is a journal, manual and guide. It is informative and engaging. It is a true and delightful original collection of verses, which relays the scenarios of Jeoffrey's success as a talented teen. The refrains convey an affirmation and message popular in his mother's generation. "Accentuate the Positive—Eliminate the Negative." It is an encouragement and a reminder to every generation.

The Adinkra African Symbols are presented in the "Become Yourself" Workshops.

ADINKRA
(Farewell)

Adinkra Symbols originate from Ghana on the Atlantic coast of Africa.

Gaana in Ashanti language.
Ghana—Warrior King

Adinkra Symbols—Proverbs, sayings, attitudes, legacy, history, philosophy, folk tales, folk songs, myths, rituals, beliefs, practices, social customs, tradition, distinct messages, specific occasions.

<u>I chose the ideals of the Adinkra Symbols for this book because</u>

<u>they are so powerful in meaning</u>.

Complementing my original thoughts, personal experiences, personal expression and life lessons.
Validating my spiritual link to current African cultures and the ancients.

BESE SAKA
Sack of Cola Nuts

Affluence
Abundance

AKOBEN

War Horn

Vigilance

Wariness

"BECOME YOURSELF"

When I was a child, I
wondered . . .
What Could I Be
An Urban Kid
An Emergency?
I'm TALL—It Has To Be
Basketball?
I'm A Sports Enthusiast
I Love Professional
Sports,
The Olympics, And
Amateur Competitions
What Could I Be
Golfer, Quarterback,
Pitcher
I'm Athletically Inclined
To Broaden
My Mind

A sack of gold would be worth a lot in most cultures. It is something rare that is used for barter and trade. A sack of cola nuts was the gold of some economies. Affluence and abundance is like money. It is also used in powerful situations, as well as, day to day affairs. When you have influence, you are in control. Your abundance should mean that you have plenty to share with others, if you also have vigilance to never give up; always stay hopeful and protect yourself, family, community and nation. Wariness balances outreach because it is necessary to be careful in a challenging environment. Urban neighborhoods can be full of threats, but emphasis on the positive encourages you to achieve your best.

It is important to feel calm and peaceful when you interact with others. Have confidence in yourself.

Journal

Class Notes

_____

_____

_____

_____

_____

_____

_____

_____

_____

_____

_____

_____

_____

_____

_____

_____

_____

_____

<u>AKOMA</u>	"BECOME YOURSELF"
The Heart	Young, Thin and Tall
Patience	I Love Basketball
	Playgrounds And Gyms
	Exercise Beams—
Tolerance	Practice Teams
	We Can Wish, We Can Dream
	Do The Work To Manifest It
<u>ADINKRAHENE</u>	I Created Another Way
	To Be All I Could See
	In My Future For Me
Chief of Adinkra	Do The Work To Manifest It
Symbols	
	The World Is Like A Mall
	You Love To See It All
	Study Now And Win
Greatness	Travel Aims—Pro Games
Charisma	We Can Wish, We Can Dream
	Do The Work To Manifest It

It can take a long time to determine, and then to achieve your wishes and dreams. You must work toward your goals by planning. In order for a good plan to work, you must study. Patience is developed by time. You must have tolerance for the mistakes of your own life. You must have tolerance for the differences of others and how those differences may or may not have an impact on your life. Many people have role models or other people that they look up to. This can be motivating. But there are other methods. One way is to actually visualize yourself at your destination. You can be your own hero. You can achieve your greatness by creating a personal future where you are in charge of bringing your best. Who you become must be an inner accomplishment that needs no outside approval.

You can be proud of good choices when they are thoughtful and work well for you.

Journal

Write your journal alongside the story

Class Notes

_____

_____

_____

_____

_____

_____

_____

_____

_____

_____

_____

_____

_____

_____

_____

_____

_____

_____

List your NEEDS. I must have the following in order
to_____.
1
2
3
4
5
6

List your WANTS. I would like to have the following
because_____
1
2
3
4
5
6

The WORK that I must do to manifest what I need and want:
(What are your educational goals?)

Journal

Write your journal alongside the story

Class Notes

_____
_____
_____
_____
_____
_____
_____
_____
_____
_____
_____
_____
_____
_____
_____
_____
_____
_____
_____

How media influenced me:

_____

_____

_____

_____

_____

_____

_____

Why:

_____

_____

_____

_____

_____

_____

_____

Other Influences:

_____

_____

_____

_____

_____

_____

_____

Journal

Write your journal alongside the story

Class Notes

_____

_____

_____

_____

_____

_____

_____

_____

_____

_____

_____

_____

_____

_____

_____

_____

_____

_____

_____

AKOMA

NTOSO

Linked Hearts

Understanding
Agree

"BECOME YOURSELF"

Linked Hearts unite with
Understanding
And Agree
    I Love To Write
    I Love To Think
    I Love To Read
    A SPECIAL
CORRESPONDENT
    Is What I'll Be
I'll Be A Special
Correspondent
    No Less—
That's Me!

Common goals can link you to another. Who do you choose for friends and associates? When you have values and character in common, you are linked hearts. Loving to write sports commentary linked Jeoffrey Best to an industry of sports writers and on-line Blogs. He could agree on particular points of view regarding games, teams or scores. He could also debate or take exception to a viewpoint. *Needs* are things you must have to survive. *Wants* are things that you would like to have and enjoy. It is important to have an understanding of what is necessary to participate in a chosen field of work. It is necessary to consider your abilities. Know your possibilities. Make a list. Choose the best. Don't settle for the lowest common denominator. Going along and fitting in, may not be the best choice. Look at the consequences of your actions, before you make a decision. Your choices are important. If you do not know why another person came to a different decision than yours; you can be strong in your own position, take time to study another viewpoint, or compromise if it is for the greater good. Find out what appeals to you and why. Find out what motivates you and why. Strive for and achieve your personal best. Learn from others, understand others. Negotiate agreements. Don't repeat negative behavior.
Families work together and pass down skills and trades.

Journal

Write your journal alongside the story

Class Notes

Fill in the blanks now. Begin the process and continue to improve. You have the choice to continue to think or to write about your concerns. Life is a process. Arrive at the answer.
It may take time to progress to the answer.

Start the sentence with: I can improve my life . . .

_____
_____
_____
_____
_____
_____
_____

Who appreciates me?

_____
_____
_____
_____
_____
_____
_____

Who helps me?

_____
_____
_____
_____
_____
_____
_____

Journal

Write your journal alongside the story

Class Notes

_____

_____

_____

_____

_____

_____

_____

_____

_____

_____

_____

_____

_____

_____

_____

_____

_____

_____

_____

BOA ME NA
ME MMOA WO

Help Me and

Let Me Help You

Cooperation
Interdependence

"BECOME YOURSELF"

Because My Thinking
Turned Into Writing
I Had An IDEA For Our Country
So I wrote To President Bill
Clinton
I Suggested A Script To Support
His Election
The President Was Impressed
With My Script
And My Resume, At 15. He Wrote
Back To Me Right Away
The Personal Letter Was Signed
I Loved Every Line
A PRESIDENTIAL
COMMENDATION
Encouraged Me To See Whatever
I Wanted To Be For My Future . . .
I Love To Write
I Love To Think
I Love To Read
A PRESIDENTIAL
CORRESPONDENT
Is What I'll be
A Presidential Correspondent
No Less—That's Me!

President Barack Obama was elected due in part to the large numbers of young people who voted. Democratic and Republican Presidents have honored individuals. Many Presidents have honored students, or neighborhoods.
Jeoffrey's mother motivated him because of her experience; including President Eisenhower visiting the campus of Holmes Avenue Elementary School, and President Kennedy's motorcade at her high school.

Journal

Class Notes

_____

_____

_____

_____

_____

_____

_____

_____

_____

_____

_____

_____

_____

_____

_____

_____

_____

Envy, jealousy and copying others can stifle YOU.
Do you see a celebrity as a person to imitate or admire?

_____
_____
_____
_____
_____
_____
_____

You are more than your current situation. Be liberated. Who do you like and what QUALITIES do they have? What are their VALUES? What is their CHARACTER?:

_____
_____
_____
_____
_____
_____
_____

What is your originality? Think of yourself in new ways. How can you develop?

_____
_____
_____
_____
_____
_____
_____

Journal

Write your journal alongside the story

Class Notes

AYA	"BECOME YOURSELF"
Fern	I Wanted A JOB—
	The President Opened That Door
	I Wrote To Shaquille O'Neal
	And Became Part Of His Team
	Not On The Basketball Court
Endurance	But To Me, An Even Higher Esteem
Resource	I Became Part Of His Writing Team
	A Byline On-Line
	The official SHAQ PAQ
	CORRESPONDENT

The fern is a symbol of endurance and resource. It is included in many insignias, flags and banners. Know and appreciate that you draw strength from reminding yourself of character traits through symbols. Your future is built on the past, as well as, the present that can encourage you. A job encourages you and reminds you that you are part of society. You are linked to everyone else in one way or another. We all need resources. A volunteer job could show a potential employer that you have the skills to add value to the company or that you are willing to learn. If you can start your own enterprise, then you can gain experience by working temporarily for a company. Competition can be good, but networking and cooperating with others, could be better. The world functions because we are part of the whole. You must have endurance to survive until you can determine your future. A recommendation from a teacher, neighbor, friend or previous employer can help you to get a job. In Jeoffrey's case; a Presidential Commendation helped to influence a celebrity's lawyer and management to help Jeoffrey, because he could help them, to write for their target market. He was their golden child, possessing an abundance of influence and affluence because he had vigilance and expressed his heart, the best. Endurance comes from inner determination. Value your qualities.

Jeoffrey Best was published in the official Shaq Newsletter. (Correspondent Reporting: Shaq National and International Fan Base.) Shaquille O'Neal, Official Shaq Paq Web Site Published a Photo of Jeoffrey Best, along with Jeoffrey's original On-Line Articles / Sports Commentary. By-Line: Jeoffrey Best. Shaq Paq Correspondent.

Journal

Write your journal alongside the story

Class Notes

Name your discipline. List your goals for a sport or hobby:

_____

_____

_____

_____

_____

Name your discipline. List your goals for a Job:

_____

_____

_____

_____

_____

To explore the possibilities for talents and achievements, which could lead to future work and life goals, Jeoffrey entered contests. Jeoffrey won trophies in a Personality Pageant. He impressed the judges with his Magic Act. He also won Best Dressed and a trophy for Personality / Charisma. He performed at several libraries, community centers and organizations. He learned that he liked another aspect of communication—community outreach. Instead of only *hanging out* with friends; he liked being part of the neighborhood/community centers and events including parades. He could express charisma by showcase and talent. His favorite family outings of art galleries and museums also became an opportunity and outlet for personal symbolic greatness, because he could see it expressed by artists in their portraits and other renderings. A person can be great in the way that he lives his life through principles and standards. It feels great to live without lies, guilt, shame and hurt. No soap opera drama, alone at home!

Jeoffrey worked a summer in Communications as a Cable TV Producer with his mother, Wende Best, Executive Producer—Progress Into The 21st Century Cable TV Show © Multi-Media Best Enterprises. It featured JPL-NASA scientists, and the Ulysses mission. It aired for Community Outreach to Schools. Jeoffrey also provided content to his mother's program at Kaleidoscope Radio, Hollywood, California. Presentations in library displays document many projects and events for the family collaborations of Jeoffrey Best and Wende Best.

Journal

Write your journal alongside the story

Class Notes

_____

_____

_____

_____

_____

_____

_____

_____

_____

_____

_____

_____

_____

_____

_____

_____

_____

_____

_____

_____

_____

AKOKONAN

The Leg of A Hen

Mercy

Nurturing

"BECOME YOURSELF"

I Visited My Former Schools
And Neighborhoods—
LIBRARIES—Everywhere I
Could
To Share My Good Fortune
And Encourage Students
In The Same Way The President
Encouraged Me
In The Same Way Shaq Paq
Honored Me!
Students Of Today Must Do
Their Part
Don't Allow Ridicule To Tear You
Apart
Don't Let Negatives Prevent You
From
Being SMART—Don't Keep
Secrets
Generate ENERGY—Do Your
Part
Ask For Help To Start

Each verse and attribute provides an opportunity to discuss issues and solutions. A person needs education, opportunity, employment and moral support. Raising-up a child, is an expression of help. Give someone a hand-up. Build-up a community. Successful people show compassion by nurturing others. The president of a country, a company, or a club will often pin a metal on a person to honor him. These metals, ribbons, badges, or trophies contain symbols. The symbols represent the character or achievement of the person. Symbols are ideals. Symbols represent the characteristics of the best. See the symbols in the "Become Yourself" Workshop.

Journal

Write your journal alongside the story

Class Notes

BI NKA BI
No One Should Bite
The Other

Peace

Harmony

ASASE YE DURU

The Earth Has
Weight
Divinity Of Mother
Earth

"BECOME YOURSELF"
I Went To Kazaam—
Shaquille's Movie Premiere
Where Mother Love Promoted
Me
I Achieved My Dream Before
The Legal Age,18
I Became A Writer
Recognized For My
Achievements
A CELEBRITY
CORRESPONDENT
No Less—That's Me!
I Did So Much When I
Was A Youth
But Regardless Of How Old I
Become
I am 35—Reaching Maturity

When I Become 50 Or A

100 Years Old Man
I'll Forever Know
Who I Am

Jeoffrey Best is a person who has Personal Character
Life Skills—Life Choices.

He is not a role-model or someone desiring to be a celebrity. He is a
good example of someone who made good decisions. He thought about
his actions and the impact on the world. He struggles every day with his
illness, but strives to live up to his name. Each one of us has personal
responsibility. Live the words of wisdom in this book as a daily motto.
Movie Factoid—Mother Love, a radio show host, and actress appeared in
Shaquille O'Neal's movie, Kazaam. Jeoffrey was encouraged by Mother
Love at the Premier of Kazaam. (The cast and crew's first view of the
finished film.)

Journal

Write your journal alongside the story

Class Notes

"BECOME YOURSELF" WORKBOOK
ORIGINAL TEXT—WORDS OF WISDOM
BY WENDE BEST

1
Character Building And Values
Must Be Taught From One Generation To Another To Realize The Best

2
We Are Connected To Our Essence And Intrinsic Humanity
By Achieving The Best

3
We Are Hopeful, Determined And Constantly Planning
Our Next Great Project In Order To
Change Fortune For The Best And Express The Spirit

4
Symbols, The Best Symbolic Values Providing Standards, And The
Vocabulary Of Symbols
Are An Expression Of Creativity
Informing The Generations In A Global Context

5
Our Legacy And Motto Is To Live Up To The Name, Best
By Improving In Every Endeavor,
At Each Level
"Do Your Best, Be Your Best, Try Your Best"

6
Conditioning And Discipline, Utilizing Free-Will, Determines How A
Person Reacts
To Everything Negative That Happens,
Until The Individual Can Create A More Desirable Reality

7
Success Can Be Relative And Personal—
Not Judged Or Measured By Riches Or Status

Journal

Class Notes

_____

_____

_____

_____

_____

_____

_____

_____

_____

_____

_____

_____

_____

_____

_____

_____

_____

_____

_____

_____

8

The Emphasis Is On The Life Affirming Positive Experiences
As A Choice And Result Of Effort To Endeavor
Live A Stress-Free Effortless Lifestyle
Each Day . . . One Day At A Time . . . For As Many Days As Possible

9

It Is Important To Share Wisdom For A Legacy

10

Self-Defined Great Projects, Special Moments, Worthwhile Events
Become A Purpose And A Path To Advancement

11

Every Life Must Matter And Have Worth, In The City, State, and Nation

12

Participation And Process Has Its Rewards
Productive Activity is Fulfilling
Values Are Riches

13

It's Too Easy To Dismiss Struggle, Because It Can Weaken You
Struggle Can Be A Process To Solve Problems And Move On
Avoid Danger—Beware Of Pitfalls—But Resolve Issues

14

Celebrate Each Step That You Make . . .
On Your Inner Journey
In The World
With Friends And Relatives
Feel Joy—Congratulate Yourself !

Journal

Write your journal alongside the story

Class Notes

_____

_____

_____

_____

_____

_____

_____

_____

_____

_____

_____

_____

_____

_____

_____

_____

_____

_____

_____

_____

"BECOME YOURSELF" WORKBOOK
ORIGINAL TEXT—WORDS OF WISDOM
BY WENDE BEST

15

The Belief That Wonderful Things Are Possible And Attract Like A
Magnet Gives Strength
Positive Belief Creates Strength
Good Energy Creates Momentum And Increases
Momentum Increases Good Moods
Good Moods Increase Stability
Good Thoughts Create Good Moods

16

Whether you have Both Parents, One Parent In Your Life,
Or No Parents—You Have A Destiny

17

Honor Your Potential Increasingly

18

Elevate Your Appreciation Of Your Own Humanity
Whether You Have Perfect Health
Marginal Abilities Or Desperate Situations

19

Discern What Is Good And Right For You

20

Eliminate Baseless Or Irrational Fear
Eliminate Condemnation

21

Be Free!
Exercise Your Right To The "Pursuit Of Happiness"
Don't Fear, Hate, Worry, Complain—Be Happy Indeed!

Journal

Write your journal alongside the story

Class Notes

"BECOME YOURSELF" WORKBOOK

TOPICS FOR DISCUSSION

Language	Summarize the development of languages as it relates to cultural values.
Memory	Discuss memory as it relates to cultural identity. Impact of cultural disconnects. Lost civilizations.
Stress	Discuss and Explain how decisions are influenced by stress.
Emotion	Discuss and Explain the impact of positive emotions for good outcomes.
Ambiguity	Discuss misunderstandings, caution / fear / paralysis
Morals	Decision Making processes
Socializing	Isolation vs. Interaction
Dysfunctional	Behaviors and Treatments
Decisions	Consequences

Journal

Class Notes

_____

_____

_____

_____

_____

_____

_____

_____

_____

_____

_____

_____

_____

_____

_____

_____

_____

_____

_____

"BECOME YOURSELF" STRESS PERCEPTION CHART NOTES

Date, Event, Duration   *Type of Stress*

DAILY: SUN.
DAILY: MON.
DAILY: TUES.
DAILY: WED.
DAILY: THURS.
DAILY: FRI.
DAILY: SAT.

WEEKLY:
WEEKLY:
WEEKLY:
WEEKLY:

MONTHLY:

Identify a specific event / occurrence of stress. Change your life by turning your attention to an emphasis on the positive.

Chart your stress for at least one month. You may be surprised to know that you actually experience less stress in terms of the amount of time involved in a particular stressful event. Your perception of a stressful life may involve magnifying the stressful event by the time you spend remembering it, replaying it over again in your mind and worrying about the event long after it is over. Living in the moment and letting go, will remind you that most of your time is stress free. The emphasis is on appreciating all of the time you experience without a stressful event occurring.

Stress Levels:

Momentary = 1 minute to 59 minutes   One Hour = 60 minutes
duration of an actual event

Half Day = More than 1 hour. Chart the actual time.   All Day = More than 4 hours

Notes = Chart the Severity from Mild to Extreme in Notes . . .

Your *Perception* of Severity may vary or differ from others

Journal

Class Notes

"BECOME YOURSELF" WORKBOOK

VOCABULARY

Perseverance Manifest	*will . . .*
Reflection Integrity	*shows . . .*
Overcoming Legacy	*reveals . . .*
Perspective Significance	*affects, effects . . .*
Endeavors Inspiration	*result of . . .*
Pursuits Appreciation	*need . . .*
Culminate Wisdom	*growth of . . .*
Destiny Stamina	*because of . . .*
Imprint Vigilance	*follows . . .*
Dilemmas Patience	*resolved by . . .*
Diagnosis Endurance	*requires . . .*
Heritage Resource	*is . . .*

Journal

Write your journal alongside the story

Class Notes

"BECOME YOURSELF" WORKBOOK

BUCKET LIST

Interests, Talents, Abilities, Jobs, Businesses . . .
Don't wait until the end of life, to decide your bucket list.
The things that you want to do in your lifetime!

Material Things:
*Other:

1.

2.

3.

4.

Places To Go:

1.

2.

3.

4.

Personal Attributes:
*Special:

1.

2.

3.

4.

People To Meet:

1.

2.

3.

4.

Summary:

_____

_____

_____

_____

_____

Journal

Write your journal alongside the story

Class Notes

_____

_____

_____

_____

_____

_____

_____

_____

_____

_____

_____

_____

_____

_____

_____

_____

_____

_____

_____

_____

"BECOME YOURSELF" WORKBOOKS & WORKSHOPS

"Become Yourself" Workbook. Sub-Titles/ Editions / Workshops By Wende Best
Abused . . . But Not Bankrupt—The Smart Woman's Guide
Abused . . . But Not Bankrupt—The Smart Man's Guide

STUDENT JOURNAL

NAME _____DATE_____

Tightening Your Belt Pledge:
I have strength. I can summon up resolve. I will decide to save my life.
I will be Resilient! I will be Thoughtful.

*Jeoffrey Best and Wende Best Las Vegas Chamber of Commerce
Ribbon Cutting Copyright permission granted*

About The Author

Wende Best grew up in 1950's Los Angeles, California. Her family was one of many that experienced a Disney type optimism—looking forward to a future of modern innovation in scientific approaches to everything from robotics and kitchen appliances to *concept cars and people movers*. Living as much in the future expectations, as well as, the everyday simple and casual lifestyles of fishing, camping and birthday parties.

"I have never been to Africa; however, I was taught from an early age to love Africa because it is part of my ancestry. (I am researching the specific details of my ancestry—which particular country in Africa and with technology, perhaps the city or village.) My Mother was native, born on a Choctaw reservation, likewise my grandmother and great-grandmother. Grandmother told me that some of her grandmother's ancestors traveled through the Sudan. My visions of her lineage plus my grandfather's, and my paternal great-grandfather's lineage from Canada, could become aspirations for another book. The family history includes intermarriages and migrations."

"My parents taught me to have values and character. I discovered the Adinkra recently; and realized the attributes that are in the Adinkra, are the same, as the ways that I was taught and strived to live, all of my life. I have come full circle and I can relate to Africa in a manner that is new and profound. My name, Wende, means to find your way on a path."

Wende Best is honoring the past, present and future, by sharing insight and the great Adinkra. The human race; every nationality, color, culture, and creed can learn from Africa / Adinkra.

Printed in the United States
By Bookmasters